C000099322

Reflections
of a
Bystander

DAN M. KHANNA

ISBN: 0692358293
ISBN-13: 978-0692358290

DEDICATION

To My Father

Who opened the doors of knowledge
Through the study of classics and literature
As I ventured
Into the world.

The woods are lovely, dark and deep,
But I have promises to keep,
And miles to go before I sleep,
And miles to go before I sleep.

Robert Frost

CONTENTS

Prologue – The Bystander

A Personal Note - The Poet in All of Us

The Mystery Called Life   1
The Never Ending End   3
The Heart's Journey   6
The Lost Innocence   7
It is My World   9
The Edge of the Universe   11
The Karmic Journey   13
My World   17
A Shattering Humiliation   19
The Last Round   21
The Wounded Scars   22
Prayers to the Protector   23
The Two Worlds   25
No Place of My Own   27
The Treasure Beneath   29
Tears in the Blanket   32
Hugs and Kicks   34
I Ran Out of Time   36
When Life Ends   38
The Chapter   39
My Life   40
The Sinking Life   41
What Will It Be?   42
Wrong Turn   43
My Life as a Human   45
If I Were Alive Today   46
The Defeat of Death   47
The Faith   49
The Emptiness   50
My Future is Me   51
The Call of the Wild   53
The Twilight   54
Love Among the Ruins   56

The Spring of Discontent   57
The Remains of the Future   58
Time to Give Up   60
Love is a Mirage   61
The Illusion of Love   62
The Passion   63
Crying for Fun   64
The Moment   65
The Hopeless Romantic   66
My Mother in Me   67
Destined to be Alone   68
The Race With Death   69
The Dangling of Hope   70
On Father's Day   71
Father's Day   72
The Sunrise   73
The End is Near   75
The Wasted Life   76
The Book of Mistakes   78
The Slowly Sinking Ship   80
The Damaged Spirit   82
From Here to Eternity   83
The Family   85

In Retrospect Revisited

PROLOGUE – THE BYSTANDER

"All the world's a stage,
And all the men and women merely players."
"As You Like It" – William Shakespeare

The universe is expanding. Our world spins and goes around. I am standing still. I see the caravans crossing the desert. I see the ships sail over oceans crossing continents. I see people all around trying to make a living and just struggling to survive. Our world is a stage where myriads of stories are told and players play their parts. There is so much to see, so much to observe, so much to learn, so much to experience, so much to think, and so much to write. There is enough fodder for the poet. The poet gives imagery, his thoughts and feelings to paper, words for the audience.

In my travels across the countries and continents I met many people who enriched my life and guided my thoughts. I will never forget.

My journey continues.

Dan Khanna

A PERSONAL NOTE

- THE POET IN ALL OF US -

"The poets are the interpreters of gods," thus spoke Socrates, the great Greek philosopher. Whether that is true or not, we will never know. But, poets and their poetry have been a significant part of our life, culture and history. From Homer, Dante, Milton, Tennyson, Browning, Keats, and thousands of poets until today they continue to enrich our life. Our modern life may not value poetry as once were true, but, people still continue to read and write poetry as a reflection of life.

There is a poet in all of us trying to express our thoughts about the life and world around us, past, present and future.

Many consider poetry the highest form of artistic expression. It comes from the soul, from within us. The poet observes the world in which he lives: its triumphs, its failures. The poet sees the life humans live, successes and failures, achievements and struggles, joys and sadness; a full fodder of inspiration that inspires the poet take the pen to compose and share thoughts, feelings and emotions with the world.

Poems are a reflection of the time and world in which we live, both good and bad. But, it is our world. We live in it for we have no alternative, at least, not yet. We talk about it. For that is life. We live it, experience it, learn from it, share it, and poets want to share. Such is the life of a poet. We are all poets, whether we write poems or not. There is a poet in all of us.

Dan Khanna

November 27, 2014

THE MYSTERY CALLED LIFE

Is life a mystery?
In many ways, it is.
Are we a mystery?
Maybe, we are.
When innocent people
Get ravaged by the storm
To lose everything they have
Why them?
Why at all?
Nature
Powerful
Unpredictable
Comes in all forms
Earthquakes, volcanoes, hurricanes, disease
Why?
Is it the price of living on this planet?
A ball
Out in the wilderness of the universe
Rotating and revolving
In space
By forces
It does not control
Just like us
Who have no control
Over the forces of nature
And over our earth
Just rotating and revolving
At the whim of an unknown force
Tumbling and regrouping
To stand
To stand still
To stand and walk
To walk, where?
For all directions
Reach someplace
We travel
We return

We go up
We come down
The forces around us
Envelop us
Why?
What do we do?
We fight humanity
To feel that we are powerful
Against natural forces
We kill our own kind
To prove ourselves
But powerful against what?
While we kill our own kind
Nature kills us
Reminding us
That we are weak and vulnerable
But do we learn?
No
That is a mystery
The inability of humans
To learn from nature
To behave in a manner
That enhances humankind
But we degrade humankind
And nature
Continues to train us
Trust us
Nurture us, nourish us
But, we go on
Without fathoming
The true nature of life and the universe
That is a mystery
And, it will
Remain a mystery.

THE NEVER ENDING END

When does end
End?

A child is born
It enters the world
It ends its existence
In the mother's womb
It ends one existence
To start another journey.
What is end?
What is beginning?
A child lives
Adjusts to life
Learns from world
And begins to create a new world
As a child becomes an adult
What ends?
Innocence
Hope
Faith.

What begins?
Desire
Ambition
Struggle
Survival.

What ended?
What began?
An existence.
We live
We enjoy

We feel the joy
We feel the sorrow

We have family
We live alone
We make it
We exist
We are at the top
We are at the bottom
Then comes an end
To a living life
To a life of contemplation.

I have lived and made it
I have lived and not made it
One life has ended
Another begins
Which is which?
No one knows
And then it starts
The end of end
The finality of existence
We anticipate
We plan
We dread
We long
But it comes
The end of all ends
When all ends meet
And diverge
Into a different path
For all paths are a beginning and an end

The end looks at us
Why are you here?
We are confused
What are you asking?

We have reached our end
We want our scorecard
Of our life
Will that be the end
Or will it be the beginning?

THE HEART'S JOURNEY

It hurts to think
That once I loved
And was loved.

That's what I believed
It was a beautiful feeling
Of faith and healing
It was a journey
Through the heart.
But it hurts to think
That I am alone
In the journey of the heart
Now that I have no love
Looking ahead
To an unknown space
Where I will be alone
Without love
The journey of heart
Has its moments
Moments of pleasure and pain
I would still make the journey
No matter what the consequences
Because
I would rather love
Then go without loving
For that is the journey of the heart.

THE LOST INNOCENCE

A child
An innocent child
Looks at the world
And wonders
Why am I here?
What will I do?
What is the future?
There are dreams
There are hopes
The child is innocent
With innocent dreams
Of good and nice

Of pleasant and love
Of living in a world
That is just like his world
Pure and innocent
Trusting and caring.

Then living starts
Reality sets in
The world is not innocent
It molds you
Transforms you
To deal with
Greed and selfishness
Callousness and arrogance
Innocence loses ground
The dreams become
Survival
Hope and faith become
Desires and ambitions

Dignity is lost
And so is innocence

The child becomes
Masses
Just like you and me
Trying to carve a living
In a unworldly world
Missing the innocence of
A world
That the child dreamt of.

The child still dreams
But is now an adult child
Living for the future
Dreaming of the past
To his innocent
View of the world
Wondering what happened
The shift
Like a razor's edge
From innocence
To skepticism
The innocent child
Is no longer an innocent child
Somehow during life's journey
The child lost it
Just like you and me,
The masses.

IT IS MY WORLD

My new world
A world
That I must create
In which I am happy, contended and satisfied.

A world that sees everything
With love
Love of people
Love of life
Love of nature
Love of being
Alive
It is a true world
Where one is one
Where one is nature
Where one is past
Where one is future
It is a continuum
A world
That is uniquely
Yours
A world where you are you
Where you are one with yourself
A world
Where you are fulfilled
A world that makes you grow
A world that makes you rich
A world that transports you into the future
The future
For which you are making the world
The future
That holds your happiness
The future that fulfills your dreams

It is for the future
That you create
A new world
A world
That makes your future a reality
And makes life
Worth living.

THE EDGE OF THE UNIVERSE

I stand at the
Edge of the universe
Gazing at our world
That spins rhythmically.
I see it
But I am not part of it
For I was thrown off
Our world
A long time ago
Hurled into space
To the end of the universe
Where one world ends
And another begins
It is an edge
That separated the past from the future
It is a chance
To observe oneself
In the grand scheme of things
Where I stand
Where I fit
Did I ever fit?
I am here alone
Surrounded by worlds
That are moving in all directions
Am I moving with them?
Or do I just see them passing by?
Am I part of them?
Or am I just an observer?
Will I move with them?
Or, be left behind?
I don't know.

I am a bystander
Waiting for the Divine Hand
To show me the path
Which I must travel
Alone with someone
Which road to take?
Where will it lead?
Where will it end?
Will it end
Or, will it go on forever?
Questions?
But no answers.
Answers elude me
But the view is magnificent
It is all there
Good and bad
Happy and sad
Beauty and ugly
But it is there.
I stand and look
And wonder
When will I be part of this universe?
This world?
Or will I remain an outsider?
A bystander
On the edge
Of the universe.

THE KARMIC JOURNEY

It begins at birth
The physical journey
But not the spiritual
One seeks material success
Other, the quest
To know thyself
The physical
Grows
In power and stature
Leaving the spiritual behind
For I am in control
Of my life
World
My destiny
I am responsible for my actions
For I am alone
Accountable to me
I am me.

The Spirit watches
In awe and patience
Knowing that someday
The physical will stop
Ponder and question
Who am I?
What have I done?
Where have I been?
How will I answer the Divine?
It has no answers
It has lived, enjoyed, and existed
But never fulfilled
An empty well.

But the Spirit is always there
Was there
Is there
Will be there

It watches
Your karmic journey
As you fill your well
With treasures
That are yours alone
And will stay with you
Even when you are gone
We all have such treasures
That we adorn once
To glitter and shine
At the few moments
And events of life
To be neatly
Tucked away in the well
For the next episode of life
The Spirit watches
Waiting patiently
For you to stop and ask
What have I done?
Where have I been?
What can I show myself
That I am proud of?

The Spirit answers
That you have been on a karmic journey
That was destined for you
To learn and experience
The journey of life and existence

But while you were on that journey
You left Me behind
Though I was with you
All the time
You chose to ignore Me
For you were the master
Of your destiny
You never asked Me
Where to go?
What to do?
It is I
That has journeyed with you
Through times and travels
Of lives and ages
It is I
Who knows you
More than you know yourself
I am still here
Your Protector, your Guide
If you chose to listen and learn
For I know the truth
About you and your journey
And I create your path
That befits you and moves you
To know Me
You must lose your physical existence
And trust Me
I have been longer than you
Than your physical existence
The physical is just a temporary phase
The true journey is to
Know your spiritual journey
For only it can fulfill you
And give you peace

Yes, it begins at birth
The journey
The physical will end with death
But spiritual goes on
And that is
The karmic journey.

MY WORLD

I live
In my world
Than is so different
Then the world
That I live in
The two worlds
One mine
Other theirs
One real
Other unreal
I live in both worlds
Trying to integrate
The real with unreal
I thought
That I would be part
Of just one world
That I was born into.

But as I grew
I created my own world
Hoping that my world
Would be compatible
With the outside world.

Time and living
People and experience
Make you a different person
Your values
Your beliefs are molded
And shaped in your mind
That creates an image
Of the world
What it ought to be.

Then you wise up
And observe the world
You live in
And question
What is the matter?
The two worlds
Are drifting apart
One being the real you
The other
An artificial survival
As time goes on
The drift
Becomes a chasm
That requires a bridge
To transverse
But not meet
The parting
Is forever
Yet one needs
A bridge
To walk
To and forth
Across worlds
To exist and survive
That's what I do
Live in my world
And exist in another world.

A SHATTERING HUMILIATION

I was on top
Of a world with loose glass
An illusion of real
Yet walking on shaky ground
The walls tumble
The earth gives way
I fall and fall
'Til there is nothing left
To hold me
Except life.

I am at the bottom of the pit
With no rungs
To climb
It is a home
Where humiliation
Meets reality
A shattering of dreams and ideals
I can't even go down
What a situation!
No more downs
Just uplifts
To what?
Beaten and bruised
With no desire
Life goes on

I have to watch it
What can I do?
Rise
Claw my way up

Not knowing
What is in store
Where is the light
Where is the beginning
When is the end
It is a climb
To reach the rim
And search for a reason
Why I am there
What got me there?
A desire to live
Or a desire to die
They are the same
For when the humiliation
Grounds you to dust
We run
To build a dust storm
That shapes our direction
And our goals
We are what we are
Hopes for the future
In a world
Where are dreams
Are shattered
And we
Rise from the ashes.

THE LAST ROUND

The last round
Of life
Is tough and final
It is make or break
You win or you lose
It is the thrill
To fight
To the end
The last round
Is your fight for survival
The fight is brutal
Vicious and hurting
But you must win
For to lose
Is your end
And you cannot
End

THE WOUNDED SCARS

The scars of life
Of friendships
Of love
Illuminate me
Shining with a glow
To remind me
Of existing in a world
That prides itself
On inflecting wounds
That scar you for life.

But scars are good
They remind you
That you live
In a world
That is not perfect
And with people
Who are not human
We just accept the frailties of this world
And accept the scars
That shape us
Each scar has a meaning
Each scar has a story
A notch, a groove
That tells of survival and existence
The wounds are real
The scars are real
They are now you
You are
The wounded scars.

PRAYERS TO THE PROTECTOR

It was a life
That I would not have survived
Without You
You were there
When I was not listening
You were there
When I was traveling the wrong path
You were there
When I was a sinner
You were there
When I was blasphemous
You were there
Watching me
Protecting me
When I didn't deserve it
I could have ended
I could have died
But, You were there
To take care
My soul
My body
My mind
You were with me
You were inside me
Nurturing me
Soothing me
Letting me cry
To shed my pain
You consoled me
When I was alone
You were there

When I didn't want You
You were there always
And I am glad
You were there.

THE TWO WORLDS

I live in two worlds
One real, one unreal
One reality, one a dream
Which is true
I don't know
Neither do I want to know
For what is the purpose?
I still have to exist
Which ever world
Makes me happy
Is my real world.

But then reality hits me
I have to choose
Between worlds
That I don't want to choose
I am pulled apart
Between living
And not living
What to do?
I examine my two worlds
One says, make money
Other says, pursue your dreams
One says, settle down
Other says, seek adventure
One says, become stable
Other says, why?
The conflict goes on
I am in the middle
Pulled in both directions
That are both appealing
And both discomforting
What do I do?

Spread my life
Like an eagle
Soar above the world
Where the world looks one,
Like a huge mass
That is interconnected
With land, water and vegetation
With mountains, valleys and rivers
With people
Big and small
Clustered and scattered
In buildings and in huts
In towns and in villages
All trying to survive in nature.
But, I am the eagle
Soaring above
Watching, observing, learning
Preparing to land
Somewhere and someplace
Where I am one
And not in the two worlds
Is there such a world
Or is it just my imagination
That the two worlds are one
Or one world is two
I don't know
So I continue to soar
Above worlds
Not knowing whether
One is two
Or two is one.

NO PLACE OF MY OWN

I live
Without a place
In a home
That is not my home.

What is home?
A place for shelter?
A place to eat?
A place to enjoy?
A place to feel secure?
A place to entertain?
A place to welcome?
A place to grow?

Yes, I have grown
But not in my place.
I have eaten
But not in my place.
Enjoy, secure and welcome
What, where and whom?
What is that?
I don't know.
The charity of others
Has it killed security and welcomeness?
The obligations
Burden my soul
As I gather the dust
And hold on to earth
To salvage sand
To build a castle
Of my dreams

27

From dust, from nowhere
A place that is my own
Small and smelly
Dirty and desolate
Empty but rich.
That is a place.
That is my place
A place of my own.

THE TREASURE BENEATH

The treasures
Are hidden
In dungeons
Beneath the sea
In deep caves
And mysterious caverns
We hunt them
To enrich ourselves
To get us out
Of our present
Leaving a world of
Fame and fortune
To be loved
And be respected
For our outward show
Affluence and ornamental structures
It is a show
Of hollowness
For the treasure we seek
Is within us
It is our foundation
That we weaken
By building
Elaborate structures
That portray
What we are not
And hide
What is within
It is a structure
To impress the world
But not ourselves

As time goes on
We build more structures
More ornaments
And further
Weaken our foundation
Ourselves
'Til we are
A huge building
A giant structure, hollow inside
That is about to crumble
Then we prop it up
With more structures
To secure
Weaknesses
To discover one day
That we are in an empty building
Alone and lost
Trying to find
A way out
The process starts
Tearing down
All walls
All structures
To strip ourselves
Of the exterior
To search the interior
Of our ourselves
To start with the
Foundation
Of our heart and soul
Of our responsibility
To ourselves
That we need to build
It is ourselves that needs love

It is ourselves
That needs cultivation
It is ourselves
That needs growth
We start at the basics
Just like kids
At the first day of school

Learn, to grow
To build ourselves
As humans with soul
With spirit
With energy
With love
To create
A foundation
And a structure
That is lasting
That is our treasure
It's the treasure,
The treasure beneath.

TEARS IN THE BLANKET

I cry
The tears cascade
Down my face
Rubbing and streaming
On my face
As they
Surrender
To the warmth
Of my blanket

Alone at night
Thinking of my past
My parents
And wondering
About my youth
My follies
My loves
And yearling for life
That I never had

Today
I cover myself
With a blanket
Of my mistakes
That shrouds my body
Into a living corpse
Of life that never
Came to life
And withered
In the sunshine
Of my dreams

The tears
Heavy and wet
With the burdens of existence
Of a wasted life
Where the yearning for death
Enveloped
The desire to live
The solace of tears
The soothing wetness
The caress of stillness
Slowly creeping
Down my face
To the soft blanket
Where they rest
Die and dry
I fall asleep
With my tears
Soaked in my blanket

HUGS AND KICKS

I am God's toy
He hugs me
And holds me to His bosom
To give me faith,
Protection and love.

Then He kicks me
When I make wrong choice,
When I make mistakes
When I disobey Him
Just like a child
Who adores and punishes
His toy
For the toy is
An extension of child
His thoughts
His deeds
And play.

God plays with me
For He adores me
He cannot do without me
For I am His extension
His extension
Of His thoughts
And belief in life
He wants me to be
Perfect
Just like Him

He is upset
He punishes me
To teach a lesson
At the same time
Protecting me
To teach me

I remain His toy
To be loved
And rejected
Just as a child
And His toy
I accept
I like
For I would
Rather be
God's toy
And accept
His hugs and kicks
That is love.

I RAN OUT OF TIME

I ran out of time
Trying to fulfill my dreams
Now I stare
At a blank existence
Empty and vacant
Devoid of happiness
And fulfillment

I wish I had more time
To do it again
Learn from my mistakes
And not repeat them
Learn from my sins
And not do them again

But time
Moves in only one direction
Forward
With living memories
Of the past
Haunting the present
Reminding me
What I lost
Where I lost
When I lost

Asking me
To mend my ways
To make a better world
For myself.

But now
Time has run out

I am in the twilight of my life
Young at heart and mind
Adjusting to an aging body
The nature is real
And cruel
The inevitable does happen
The end.

But, I am not ready
So much to do
So little time
I do have dreams
And always will
I just
Ran out of time.

WHEN LIFE ENDS

When life is about to end
It seeks to prolong itself
Afraid of the future

And unknown
What it may bring
Afraid
To cut the umbilical cord
That connects
Life to eternity
To a world
Where all is at peace
A world where we all go
To escape from the life
That we all live
In a world
That accepts us
But where we do not belong
It is no use to prolong
What is inevitable
Better and decent
A true reality.

THE CHAPTER

Life is
A series of chapters
That change with the landscape
Writing each episode
Some are long
Some are short
Some are boring
Some are exciting
Some are happy
Some are sad
And, some are shocking

Yet each chapter is unique
And keeps the book of life
Engrossing and a page-turner
Each chapter ending
But continuing on to the next
It is never ending
'Til the final chapter

Which is always
The end of life
Or is it?
Or does it continue
To the next life?

Will it ever end?
We do not know
And when the
Last chapter happens
We never know.

MY LIFE

My life
Is in search of life
Trying to find
What I keep losing
What I lost years ago.

Is it my present life
that eludes me?
Or the future life
that folds to unfold?

So I reflect
On my life as a human
A human that is a victim of life
Or, is it, my life
That is shaping
My humanity.

THE SINKING LIFE

My life is like a
Sinking ship
That slowly swallows water
To reach its
Final resting place
The bottom of the ocean
Where it will find
A stable floor
To hold it
Unlike the ups and downs of the ocean
Just like my life
That went through
Undulating motions
To the moods of the ocean
With no land in sight
To be left
To nature
To suck the life
Of the ship
And sink it
To its final resting place.

WHAT WILL IT BE?

A new life
A new love
New friendships
A new direction

Or, will it be
The same
Old stale life
That seems to go
In no direction
Just stays there
'Til I get drained

And forces me
To just survive

Now, I am here
So what will it be?
Where will I be?
Moving on
Or remaining still
Only life will tell.

WRONG TURN

Sometime, somewhere
In my life
I took a wrong turn
That took me
On journeys
That I had not planned
For all my plans
Went into disarray
And each plan
Resulting in new plans
All plans
Falling by the wayside.

My life took a turn of its own
Unknown to me and to my life
I traveled on journeys
That crisscrossed
Continents
Into unchartered waters
Wandering into an open sea
With no land in sight
Depending on intuition
To guide my soul.

My journey became turbulent
As waves crested me
And drowned me
Like a roller coaster
Got tossed around
At its whims and moods
And that ups and downs
Seem flat to me

I had no idea
Where I was being lead.
I drifted with a purpose
To find land
Where I could stand
And find my path.

Should I seek my original path?
Or find a new path
To unknown new places?

But the wrong turn
Has wasted so much of my life
Or has it enriched me
With the lessons of life
To prepare me for a new journey.

Have I learned, or
I just felt lost.
It depends
On how I view my life
Whether the wrong turn
Was a mistake, or
Divine guidance
Only time will tell.

But, I have ways to go
To learn
Whether the wrong turn
Was self-inflicted, or
A Divine nudge.
'Til then
I just go on
The path
Of the wrong turn.

MY LIFE AS A HUMAN

My life as a human
Is in search of life
While the life
Is searching for
The human in me
And the human in me
Is searching for life

Will the two meet
Or run on parallel paths
Staring at each other
But never meeting
Two aliens
At odds with each other

One emotional
Other devoid of emotions
Where is the balance
Of nature
The human dancing with life
In an awkward embrace
Keeping the rhythm
But out of step

The dance goes on
'Til the human passes
Leaving life alone
To search
For a new partner
And continue
The dance of life.

IF I WERE ALIVE TODAY

If I were alive today
What will I do with my life?
Will I ask to prolong it?
Or, will I ask it to end?
Or, will I let it continue
With its ups and downs
And accept
Whatever comes my way?
Let Divine justice
Sort it out for me
Leaving me alone
To exist
As an insignificant
Part of the universe.
Such is life.

THE DEFEAT OF DEATH

Yes, I defeated death
At least for a while
Though, I know
It will eventually get me
But, for the moment
Let me enjoy
The joy of winning.

I have fought it
And pushed it away
Vanquished it
And I take pride in my victory
To gain strength
To face
Its onslaught again
I know it will come
It will attack forcefully
For it does not like to lose
Strange, for in the end

It eventually wins
But, I will not let it win easily
I will fight it every step
And, not just push it back
But enjoy the glory
Of the triumph
Every battle victory
That comes my way
It is just acceptable
On its own terms
But, we will determine the end
We will decide
When death can take us

For then we are the masters
And death will have to accept that
It will have no choice
It will have no say
We will tell it
We are ready
Now take us
And in that glory
Is the defeat of death.

THE FAITH

Faith is required
To make it through life
Faith in oneself
In God
In love
In our values
In others

Theses combinations of faith
Is essential for life
To make it through
With its ups and downs
With its good and bad
If you have faith
In yourself
That life is ordained
And God is watching over you
But it all will pass
One way or another
If you have faith
In yourself
And people
Who believe in you
For in the end
It is just you
And people
Who love you
Just thank them
You will succeed
Let faith guide you.

THE EMPTINESS

The emptiness in me
Expands to cover my senses
Shrouds me
In a curtain of despair
And helplessness
That makes me
Wonder about life
About me
And, what about me
Creates the emptiness.
Do I know it?
Where do I find the answer?
Within me
Or, outside?
Outside where?
The answer has to be
Within me
But, I don't know it.
Where does it reside?
My mind?
My heart?
I search in the emptiness
Groping for an object
That I cannot find
Emptiness in emptiness
Just like life.

MY FUTURE IS ME

My future is me
No one can make it for me
No one can destroy it for me
I am my own destiny
My guide
The wisdom of the ancient
The wisdom of my parents
The experience of life
That is all I have
But, I can extract
Good memories
Knowledge and learning from it
And build a foundation
That is strong
As the pyramids
To withstand
The onslaught of time
On this living structure
But, I have the strength of the past
And wisdom of the masters
To guide me in the future
The future is mine
It depends on what I want
The foundation is there
The monument
I have to create
I have to design
I have to build
Build to my liking
Build to my taste

A future that is bright
That is hope
A future I can be proud of
When the end comes
I can say
I did a great job
I am proud of me
I am the future.

THE CALL OF THE WILD

There is a call for me
From the wilderness
Asking me to come
To the unknown
Where fate awaits me

It is a call
That I cannot ignore
For it is the call of the wild
Far away
Beckoning me
To share in the future
That I do not know
The destiny that eludes me
And the wild that surrounds me

I will go
For that is my destiny
To seek a path
That fate has prepared for me

Where it leads
I don't know
Where it ends
I don't care

For it is the path of life
Which we all must journey
To reach the end
Where all ends end
And a new future starts
I go
And surrender to its call
The call of the wild.

THE TWILIGHT

I stare at the twilight of my life
Reflecting on its colors
Dark and bright
Wondering
What my end will tell the world
A life of profit or loss
What will my obituary say?
Will I even have an obituary?
Or will I fade into oblivion?
Alone and forgotten
Or will my obituary say
All the good things
That I did not do
A loving father
A family man
Was I?
People who despised me
Will either keep quiet
Or lavish praise
For speaking ill of the dead
Is not nice
Why?
Death forgives everything and everybody
Even enemies
It cleans the slate.

As I stare at the sunset
Pondering what thought
Will remain of me
If I can observe
What people say about me
After my death

That would be
A Shakespearian drama
Pathos and excitement
Divine and demons
All sharing the stage
From twilight to sunrise
Where a new dawn awaits me
Full of hope, faith and dreams
The twilight fades
And I am alone
Staring at the new sun.

LOVE AMONG THE RUINS

Love among the ruins
Can blossom the wilderness
Into an oasis
Of beauty and splendor
The same ruins
That lay desolate and lonely
Without love
Become a garden
Of colorful flowers
Scent and aroma
Abound of intoxicating feelings
Exciting adventures begin

That take us
Into journeys across
Different artful places
Into a world
Where it is just love
Just us
And then those ruins
No longer matter
For love can happen anywhere
Even in the ruins.

THE SPRING OF DISCONTENT

Spring is here
flowers are blooming
time to plant new seeds
but, there is discontent
in my life
which does not want
to plant
the seeds of failure
but stare
at the barren trees of fall

wondering
why leaves fall
and raking the leaves of life
into bags
to throw away
ignoring the birth of spring

ignoring life
refusing to blossom
and refusing to plant new seeds
that is
the spring of discontent.

THE REMAINS OF THE FUTURE

As I gaze
Into the crystal ball of my future
I see a barren shore
Laid waste
By the tides of the ocean
Groping and gnawing
At the sands of my life
Removing and depositing
Layers of age
Innocence and maturity
Ignorance and experience
Creating a new sand structure
That I do not recognize
It is not the sand
That I started with
It is not the sand
That I played with
It is not the sand
That I held
That slipped through my hand
I do not recognize
The new structure
Alone and desolate
Full of debris and filth
That mistakes and misfortunes
Of life
Piled on the beach
That I need to clean
With my bare hands
Crawling through the ruble of my life

Seeking peace
In the coarse softness of the sand
Lying down quietly
Hoping the tides will come to me

Drench me
And cover me with a new ocean
And slowly submerge me
Into the earth
And cover me with salt water
And leave me in an oblivion-peace
Alone
With the remains of my future.

TIME TO GIVE UP

When is that time
The time one feels
That it is time to go
Physically one still lives
But mentally tells oneself
That it is over
I tried
I lived
I am alive
But the curtain must fall
The show cannot go on forever
The sales are declining
The audience is thinning
The empty theatre
Is a reminder
That the show is over
There are no more spectators
The performances have ended
Actors have gone
Time to close the curtain
Time to give up
It is over

LOVE IS A MIRAGE

Love is a mirage
I see it
It is far
It is near
I will reach it
Touch it
And embrace it
And quench myself
In its sweetness
I move towards it
It moves further
I run
It runs
The faster I move
The faster it moves
I get tired
I can see it
But cannot touch it
It is there
But not there
Love is
Just like a mirage

THE ILLUSION OF LOVE

Love
Is it real
Or is it an illusion
That exists only in our minds
The reality and illusion
Are one and the same
For they both cause emotions
That we cannot control
Emotions that run us
Makes us feel things
That we don't want to feel
For that feeling
Clouds our thinking
And makes us do things
That we may regret
For love creates an illusion
That all will work out
And will be well
And happiness will prevail
And that is an illusion
The illusion of love

THE PASSION

The passion
Tempered with love
Arouses senses
That intoxicates us
And transports us
Into a world
That just belongs to us
When we become the world
Holding and touching
Embracing and caressing
The bodies
Singing with delight
As they explore each other
Trying to find spaces
Where no spaces exist
Creating new aliveness
Of wonders and feelings
That only passion can seek
Full of love
To embrace love
With its might
And crush it
Into one world
Of love and passion

CRYING FOR FUN

I cry
To feel better
To release the emotions
That pile up inside me
Gushing like a waterfall

With a roar and splatter
That spreads the feelings
All over the landscape

I feel better
The eyes dry up
I can see again
With washed eyes
The future
That still exists
That I must face
With a clarity of emotions

Now that I have cried
I must go ahead
To another time
When I will cry again
For fun

THE MOMENT

The moment
When the flow of emotions
Sparks between two hearts
Igniting a passion
That engulfs the mind and body.

When that happens,
We don't know
It just happens
We don't feel.

At that moment
When fate entwines us
Creating a new bond
Of love, feelings and warmth
That forever breaks all barriers
And makes us one soul
That then journeys together
To create a new moment
That fills our lives and bodies
With eternal love
And that is
The moment.

THE HOPELESS ROMANTIC

I love romance
Even though I don't have it
The giddy feeling
The butterflies
Staring into each other's eyes
Moist and tender
Holding hands
The gentle touch
Sharing hopes and dreams
Of a new future
Where we are one
In a world
Of our creation
Full of love and happiness.

It may be a dream
But it feels good
To think of romance
And be in love
Even if it is not there
It is me
The hopeless romantic.

MY MOTHER IN ME

I am my mother's son
A mother
Who wanted a son
To be with her
And take care of her.

She gave me wisdom
Street-smart learning
That I always did not appreciate
Yet I listened
I resented
But, I did not
Live to her expectations.

She is no longer alive

Yet, she is with me
In my thoughts
In my mind
Her stories
Her teachings
Her love
Still guide me.

She is here with me
In my soul and blood
She still takes care of me
She always will
For my mother
Is in me.

DESTINED TO BE ALONE

As the end draws near
I am still alone
Alone drinking in a bar
Alone enjoying Chianti and pasta in a restaurant
Alone watching drama in a theatre
Alone listening to opera.

Is this what I wanted?
No
I hoped I would be with someone special
But, then
When did life fulfill my dreams?

The ones I liked
Did not like me
The ones who liked me
I did not like them

The journey of
Mismatched expectations
Has left me alone
To face what is inevitable
A life of loneliness
But still rich in mind and soul.

THE RACE WITH DEATH

The end is near
The body creaking
A new world is approaching
And I still have lots to do
More to accomplish
And not die
Without a mark
Of people forgotten

Time
Has become an enemy
The body hindrance
But, the spirit
Lives and wants to live
To create
And contribute
Memories
To a world
That needs
And so must I
Continue my journey
To contribute
And meet my dreams
In the time that is left
That is
The race
Between life and death.

THE DANGLING HOPE

The hope is still there
For a life
Of romance and passion
To love someone special
Who loves you freely
To hold each other
'Til our bodies and soul
Merge into one
Such that we move in unison
To the rhythms of
Life and living
With a passion
That invigorates and ignites
Desires
To live in a world
That is so special
Full of love and contentment
Peaceful existence
In the bosom of life

ON FATHER'S DAY

On this special day
I wonder
Why is it
That makes me proud
To be a father?

It is my daughter
Who makes me proud
To be a father

She embodies
The free spirit
Of youth and the future
That makes me forget the past
And love the future

She is hope
She is faith
That a better world exists in the future
Only a father can wish
That she create a new world
That is hers
And she is happy, settled and secure
And that is all
A father can ask
She is the future

FATHER'S DAY

Today is Father's Day
A day
When children honor their fathers
With gifts, lunches and dinners
Businesses lavish gift sales
To commercialize the feelings
Do we need a special
Commercialized day
To thank our fathers?

Why can't we do it every day?
Do all fathers deserve it?

I had a father
Who is in a better world
But, I remember him every day
To me every day is Father's Day
What I am today
Is because of him
He is my father
I do not need a special day
To honor him
I honor and remember him
Every day.

THE SUNRISE

The first rays
Of light and hope
Escape the darkness
To reveal a new day
That is emerging
To seek a new beginning
Of hope and faith
To start a new day
That will change everything
Or change nothing

Will it be a day
That propels my life
In new directions
Or, will it be a day
That will fade away
Like other days
That I don't care to remember
Just a day
In the life of life

But, then it is sunrise
The rays brighten the sky
The shiny golden rays
That emit
A desire of hope
For a better world
A peaceful world
With no violence

As we awake
We are full of hopes
And then the reality of existence hits us

And we become robots
Just going around in circles
Trodding the earth
That supports us
The rays brighter the world
But our lives remain in the darkness
Still awaiting sunrise
The sunrise of our world.

THE END IS NEAR

I can feel it
I can hear
The gentle call
Reminding me
That the end is near
The body
Slowly disintegrating
The will to live ebbing
The sunset
Glaring at me
With its shining colors
Brightening the skies
With its golden rays
As it sinks
Into the ocean
To the calmness
Beneath the waters
Into a new world
Of warm coolness
The end beckons
It is near

THE WASTED LIFE

As I stand
At the precipice
Of my end
I wonder how I got here
Across barren wasteland
And unforgiving oceans
To look beyond
Into an emptiness
Of life
Beyond life
That I must venture into
To find my ultimate destiny

I reflect
As I await to jump
Into the abyss
Of what my life has been

Is it a wasted life?

I don't know
But, I do know
That my dreams shattered
My mistakes in life surround me
And bark at me
For losing all I had gained

But, the past is past
Just a reflection
Of what I wanted
And what I am

There is no turning back
As time propels me forward
To the edge
And asking me
To take the plunge
Which I will
Which I must
And what awaits me
In that emptiness
I must trust
For that is the end of my journey
An end to a wasted life

THE BOOK OF MISTAKES

Where do I start?
My first mistake
When did I make it
That started a trend
Of mistakes
In life, love and career.

Actually, it started
The day I was born
When I did not want to be born
Into this world
Where I felt
I do not belong
But, I came
To live
A life of mistakes
Disconnected from the world
And what it stands for
That was my first mistake
And then it all started
Choosing a profession
That I did not like
But needed to exist and survive
Like a materialistic soul
Ignoring my own pleas
To be an artist
Create for life
In the wisdom to succeed
I lost myself
In day to day survival
Existing in a vacuum
Without fresh air to breathe

Instead breathe recycled air
Of mediocrity
Just like the rest of the world

And then I love
For I believe in love
But love dooms me
Chips at my heart
Carving scars
That linger
Losing remnants of my heart
That propels me to live
A life without love
Facing mediocrity
In every step
Lack of wisdom
Lack of integrity
Lack of compassion
What this life offers
Must continue
It is not over
My mistakes will continue
Why not?
My life is still alive
And I have to write
My book of mistakes.

THE SLOWLY SINKING SHIP

The slowly sinking ship
Enjoys an experience

Of life and death
At the same time
It sees the oceans
That it sailed majestically
Moving peacefully
Through undulating waves
The same ocean
That kept it upright
Now wants to swallow it
Slowly but gracefully
As the ship
Scans the horizon
That is gradually disappearing
Layer by layer
It sees the expanse of ocean
And mystery of its bosom
Simultaneously
As it sinks
Slowly
Enjoying both pain and pleasure
The sensations
Overwhelm it
It cries
The water drowns it
Its tears mingle with the ocean
As it ventures into its depths
To live peacefully
At the bottom
Surrounded by calmness of nature

As it breathes its final sigh
And settles permanently
To a life of peace
The journey has ended
It is now at peace

THE DAMAGED SPIRIT

Here I am alive
Broken in spirit
And struggling
to keep pieces together
pieces of broken
spirit, emotions and fate
shattered beyond recognition
into sands of time
here I am
sifting through the sands
to find pieces of life
that I scattered away
into the winds of fate
now I stand alone
on the dunes of time
staring at the ocean
hoping to bring my pieces back
so I can start
putting them together
for fate
to break it again

FROM HERE TO ETERNITY

The distance from here to eternity
Is so small
When you measure it
In terms of time
In one split second
One can transverse across the universe
And not even realize
That one is there
I was just here
And now where am I?
I was healthy one second
I was sick in another second
What transpired inside the mind
To make the body change so dramatically?
What forces of nature were in effect?
What divine wisdom was guiding destiny?
I was alive
Very much so
And then, I could not have been
It just happens
Does that event
A result of a series of events?
Or is it just one cosmic event?
Or is it the hand of fate?
Or a warning from the soul?
Whatever it is
We don't know
We just know
That event happens

Why it happens
Remains a mystery
To us
And that is
The Hand of God

THE FAMILY

It is there
The day you are born
And it stays with you
'Til you die
The family
That you inherit at birth
It waits for you
With joy and anticipation
Welcoming you in the world
So you are not alone
To be with you
As you grow up
Guiding and helping
When you stumble
Holding and pushing
When it requires
Giving you an identity
That you belong
And are part of something big
It is not a perfect union
Neither was it intended to
But it is there
To be there
When you need
The family

IN RETROSPECT REVISITED

I am not a poet. I never intended to be one. It just happened by chance, just like many things in my life. I like to write poetry. I feel good; it makes me happy. There is so much going around in the world creating thoughts and ideas that you want to share.

It was in the 1980's when I wrote my first poem. I was very successful professionally, but I was not satisfied with my personal life and I wanted to find meaning in my life. One day, I picked up a pen and started writing. I name the result, "The Traveler", for I had been traveling for most of my life.

I have written over twelve hundred poems and I will continue to write as long as I live. Reflections of a Bystander is my second book. Life and living reveals many things about us. It is good to reflect and pen a few words to share. More books are coning. The next one is title, Mirror of the Soul.

My travels continue,

Dan Khanna

ABOUT THE AUTHOR

Dan Khanna considers himself a traveler through life enjoying an adventurous journey. Dan was born in New Delhi, India. After he completed high school, at St. Columbus High School, Dan left India striking out for California via short stays in London, Montreal and Milwaukee, Wisconsin. Although his dream was to pursue a career in the arts, acting, music, and writing, a quirk of fate placed him in engineering college and pursuing a business management career, in which he excelled. Dan completed an undergraduate program in engineering, and a Master and Doctorate in Business Administration.

Dan worked in Silicon Valley's high technology firms and was a CEO and founder of several firms. He changed careers to be a professor. Now, he again is pursuing his dream in creative endeavors.

Dan is the quintessential Renaissance Man, whose interests span the gamut of the arts, sciences, history, social and political studies, classics and philosophy. His search for knowledge began in his early life where his father was the Chief Education Officer of Delhi and his mother was a Sanskrit scholar. Dan speaks English, Hindi, Urdu, Punjabi, and Gujarati.

As a child, Dan read voraciously, particularly enjoying novels, such as Sherlock Holmes, Agatha Christie, Earl Stanley Gardener, Ian Fleming's James Bond series and classic works of Shakespeare, Tolstoy, Dickens, Oscar Wilde, Thomas Hardy, and other writers. He was very interested in poetry and read English poems of Browning, Keats, Milton, Tennyson, and Frost, as well as, other poets, while mastering Urdu poetry. His intellectual interests including studying Western and Eastern philosophers, especially Socrates, from whom he learned questioning methodology employed in his research, lectures and seminars.

During his parochial education, Dan was interested in various sports: cricket, soccer and field hockey. His love for the arts and music was honed to a level that he performed in plays, movies and solo concerts.

Dan's present journey is devoted to creative arts and activities, primarily writing poetry, fiction and non-fiction books and plays, while continuing to acquire knowledge of diverse subjects. He has published one book and has written over twelve hundred poems comprising eighteen books to date. Dan has several non-fiction and fiction books in development.

Made in the USA
San Bernardino, CA
11 January 2015